Whose Ears Are These?

A Look at Animal Ears—Short, Flat, and Floppy

Written by Peg Hall
Illustrated by Ken Landmark

Content Advisor: Julie Dunlap, Ph.D.

Reading Advisor: Lauren A. Liang, M.A.

Literacy Education, University of Minnesota

Minneapolis, Minnesota

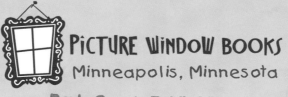

PICTURE WINDOW BOOKS
Minneapolis, Minnesota

Editor: Lisa Morris Kee

Designer: Melissa Voda

Page production: The Design Lab

The illustrations in this book were prepared digitally.

Printed in the United States of America.

1 2 3 4 5 6 08 07 06 05 04 03

Library of Congress Cataloging-in-Publication Data

Hall, Peg.

  Whose ears are these? : a look at animal ears—short, flat, and floppy / written by Peg Hall; illustrated by Ken Landmark.

    p. cm. – (Whose is it?)

  Summary: Describes how the ears of different animals look and how they function.

  ISBN 1-4048-0004-2 (library binding : alk. Paper)

  1. Ear—Juvenile literature. [1. Ear. 2. Animals.] I. Landmark, Ken, ill. II. Title.

  QL948 .H33 2003   E

  573.8'9—dc21   2002005735

Picture Window Books
5115 Excelsior Boulevard
Suite 232
Minneapolis, MN 55416
1-877-845-8392
www.picturewindowbooks.com

Open your ears and hear who's who.

An animal's ears can be long or short. Ears can be huge.
Ears can be tiny.

Look closely at an animal's ears. Ears can tell you how an animal
finds food or how it stays safe from an enemy. Some ears even
help animals stay cool when it's hot.

Ears don't all look alike, because they don't all work alike.

Can you guess who hears with these ears?

Look in the back
for more fun facts
about ears.

3

4

Whose ears are these, flapping in the heat?

These are an African elephant's ears.

The African elephant's ears are big and flat.
The ears flap like fans to keep the elephant
cool in the hot sun.

Fun fact: An
elephant uses its
ears to frighten
away enemies. It
opens its ears out
to the sides. That
makes the elephant
look bigger and
more frightening.

Whose ears are these, waving back and forth?

These are a cottontail rabbit's ears.

The rabbit's long ears stick up straight at the slightest sound. The rabbit waves its ears back and forth to find where danger may be.

Fun fact: Different kinds of rabbits have different kinds of ears. The jackrabbit's ears are even longer than the cottontail's ears. The lop-eared rabbit's floppy ears hang down the sides of its head.

Whose ears are these, listening for echoes?

These are a brown bat's ears.

A brown bat hunts at night. As it flies about, it makes clicking noises that echo back. The bat listens for the echoes to help it find its way through the dark.

Fun fact: A brown bat's ears are specially shaped to catch echoes. It can use an echo to find even a tiny bug flying by!

Whose ear is this, listening in the rain forest?

11

This is a gorilla's ear.

A gorilla's ear looks a lot like a person's ear. A gorilla has good hearing. It can hear an unwanted visitor, even if the gorilla can't see the visitor through the dense rain forest.

Fun fact: Gorillas listen for signals from other gorillas. When the male leader of a gorilla group thumps his chest, it makes a loud, hollow sound. The sound warns other male gorillas to stay out of his way.

Whose ears are these, listening for bugs in the sand?

These are a desert fox's ears.

The desert fox has big, cupped ears that catch a lot of sound. The fox can hear even an insect walking across the sand.

Fun fact: The large ears of the desert fox keep it cool. The fox's extra body heat escapes through the thin skin of the ear.

14

Whose little ear is this?

This is a sea lion ear.

A sea lion's ear is just a little flap, but a sea lion still has good hearing, even under water. It uses its ears to find prey and to stay away from enemies.

Fun fact: If a sea lion pup gets lost, it uses its ears to find its mother. Each mother sea lion makes her own singing sound. The pup listens for its mother's special song to find her.

Whose ear is this, covered with feathers?

This is a barn owl's ear.

The barn owl turns its head toward rustling sounds in the grass below. The feathers around its face direct the sound into its ears. The owl's excellent hearing helps it hunt mice in the dark.

Fun fact: The ears of a barn owl have different shapes, and one is higher than the other. That helps the owl figure out exactly where a sound comes from.

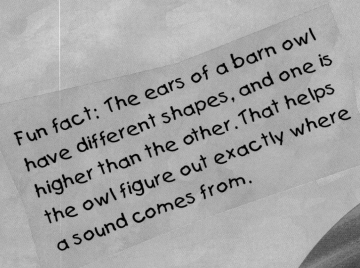

Whose ear is this, listening to a secret?

This is your ear!

Your ears catch a song from the radio or a whisper from a friend. Just like other animals, you use your ears for staying safe and finding things. Your ears don't move in different directions, like a rabbit's, but some people can wiggle their ears a little. Can you?

Fun fact: Your ears help you balance. Deep inside each ear is a special liquid. The liquid moves around when you walk or jump. Tiny hairs in your ear feel the movement and tell your brain, so you don't fall down.

How Good Are Your Ears?

Test your ears. Sit on a chair and cover your eyes with a blindfold. Have a friend stand somewhere in the same room and make a noise. Point to where you think the noise is coming from. Have your friend move to a new spot, then try it again.

How did you do? If you were a rabbit and could move your ears, this would be easy!

Fun Facts About Ears

EARDRUMS Eardrums help carry sounds to your brain. You can't see your eardrums. They are too far inside your ears. The outside part of your ear funnels sound to the eardrum. People and many animals have hidden eardrums, but the toad has flat eardrums near its eyes.

HEAR THE BIRDS Hearing is very important to birds. A bird's song, or call, is how it talks to other birds. Female birds are attracted to a male bird's song, while male birds hear it and stay away.

DOGS' EARS Dogs can hear sounds that humans cannot. That is how a dog whistle works. It makes a sound too high for a person to hear, but just right for a dog's ears.

NO EARS? A fish does not have ears on the outside of its body. Instead, sounds travel through bones and the liquid in its head.

ANGRY EARS When a horse is angry, it points both ears back. Other horses know to stay away.

EARS WITH SOMETHING EXTRA The bobcat has stiff hairs that stick out from the tips of its ears. Some people think the hairs help the bobcat hear better.

Words to Know

balance A person in balance can stand or move without falling.

brain Your brain is inside your head. It tells the rest of your body what to do.

eardrum An eardrum is a part of the ear that moves when sound hits it. The eardrum helps send sounds to the brain.

echoes Echoes are sounds that bounce off things. Echoes make sounds seem like they are happening over and over again.

liquid A liquid is something you can pour. Water is one kind of liquid.

To Learn More

AT THE LIBRARY

Arnold, Caroline. *Did You Hear That?: Animals with Super Hearing.* Watertown, Mass.: Charlesbridge, 2001.

Hartley, Karen, Chris MacRo, and Philip Taylor. *Hearing in Living Things.* Des Plaines, Ill.: Heinemann Library, 2000.

Schwartz, David M. *Animal Ears.* Milwaukee, Wis.: Gareth Stevens, 2000.

Trumbauer, Lisa. *Animal Ears.* Mankato, Minn.: Yellow Umbrella Books, 2000.

ON THE WEB

Lincoln Park Zoo
http://www.lpzoo.com
Explore the animals at the Lincoln Park Zoo.

San Diego Zoo
http://www.sandiegozoo.org
Learn about animals and their habitats.

Want to learn more about animal ears?
Visit FACT HOUND at
http://www.facthound.com

Index